GROW YOUR OWN

NASTURTIUMS

Illustrated and designed by

Ley Honor Roberts

eden project

Getting started

Jolly, orange nasturtiums are really easy to grow. They will trail nicely from a big pot, a window box or a hanging basket, or brighten up a sunny flowerbed. Start them early indoors in small containers or wait until it's warmer and sow them straight outside. Here's what you will need:

A sunny patch of earth

Seed pots

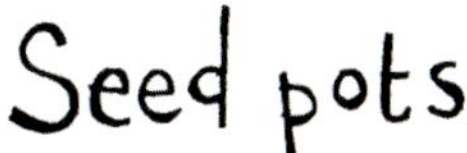

All these things make good first plant pots for seeds. Solid containers need drainage holes in the bottom.(Ask for adult help with this.)

Seed compost

Available in bags from supermarkets and garages as well as garden centres. Peat-free is best.

Gro-bags are a cheap way of buying seed compost.

Patience

The nasturtiums will take about 8 weeks to get from seed to flower. Keep a diary to see how they grow each day.

Sowing your nasturtium seeds

The best time to sow

The best time to sow is March and April indoors, or May and June outside. After midsummer, the days get shorter and the plants don't have time to reach their full height and make flowers before autumn.

planting time　　midsummer　　flowering time

| Jan | Feb | Mar | Apr | May | Jun | Jul | Aug | Sep | Oct | Nov | Dec |

What to do

1. **Either** fill your containers with seed compost.

OR ...
Wait until it's warmer and find a sunny spot in the garden. Clear away any weeds and stones.

2. Water the seed compost (in the pots) or the soil (in the flowerbed).
Make sure it is moist but not too wet – like a squeezed-out sponge.

3. Plant your seeds 15 cms
apart at twice their own depth.

If you are starting them off in egg
boxes, put one in each section.

4. Cover the seeds with seed compost (if they're
in pots) or earth (if they're in a flowerbed).

Like us, seeds need water, air and food to grow.
Your nasturtium seeds get their water and air from the soil,
and food from inside their seed coats (which is why they are quite big).
When the shoots appear above the soil, they need light too.

From seeds to seedlings

Sunlight

Once your nasturtium seeds have sprouted, make sure they have plenty of sun. If they are in pots, move them into the sunshine.

Watering

Water the seedlings so the soil or compost stays damp. That might not be every day.

If it is too wet, your seedlings will drown because they can't breathe.

If it is too dry, the seedlings could die of thirst.

If the seedlings are strong and look good, you've got the right balance.

Potting on

Once nasturtium seedlings have four little
leaves they will need more room to grow if they are in small pots.
Now is the time to plant them in bigger containers, or in the garden (if you
didn't sow the seeds outside in the first place).

Planting out your seedlings

How to plant out seedlings from small pots

Turn the pot upside down and gently pull it off the plant.
Try to keep as much soil on the roots as possible. Dig a hole and plant the
seedling in the soil at the same depth as it was in the compost. Press it in with
your fingers but be careful not to squash the stem – this is like the plant's
drinking straw for sucking up water up from the soil.

Biodegradable seed pots

Seedlings in cardboard containers like egg boxes can stay in
them, because the cardboard will rot. Separate the sections
and tear the edges a bit before putting them in the earth.

Interesting pots

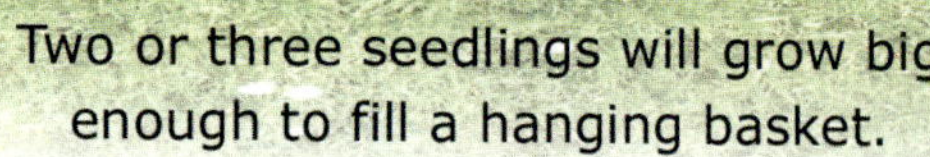

Two or three seedlings will grow big
enough to fill a hanging basket.

Friends and Foes

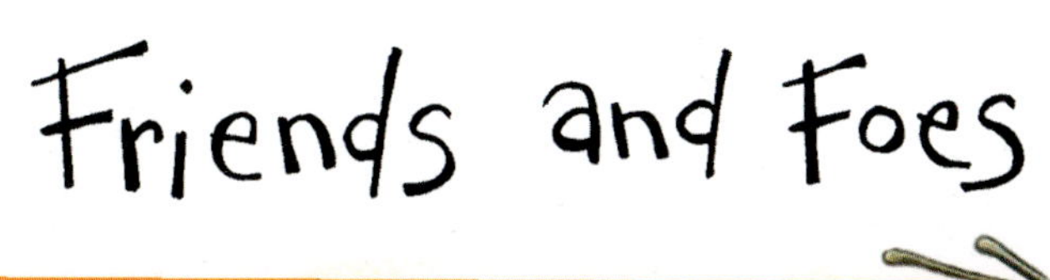

Caterpillars Some butterflies like to lay their eggs under nasturtium leaves. When the eggs hatch, hundreds of tiny caterpillars can munch their way through them. Check the leaves daily and remove the caterpillars.

Aphids Blackfly are aphids that love nasturtiums. Get rid of these pests by watering the plants with a weak solution of eco washing-up liquid. Water them with a weak solution of liquid seaweed (from a garden centre) as a tonic to help them get better. Ask an adult to help you with this.

Ladybirds are really good for your nasturtiums because they love to eat aphids. If you see any ladybirds in your garden, catch them very carefully and put them on your plants.

Worms Be gentle with worms – unlike slugs and snails, they are gardeners' friends, helping to dig the soil as they make channels through it, and helping to feed it with their poo!

Watch them grow
Spreading and trailing

Your nasturtium plants will soon spread to fill the space. As they get more and more umbrella-like leaves they will start to trail down from hanging baskets and other containers.

Soon they will be covered with bright orange flowers that close up at night. Look for dewdrops in the middle of the leaves first thing in the morning after a clear night.

Bees

The bright flowers will attract honey bees, who come to collect sweet nectar and pollen.

Watering

Water your nasturtiums if it doesn't rain.
Make sure the water goes down into the soil.
Remember that plants in pots dry out very fast.

A plant you can eat

Leaves

Another name for nasturtiums is summer watercress.
Try nibbling a young leaf. It tastes quite hot, like watercress.
You can add a few to your salad or sandwich. A nasturtium
leaf contains ten times more Vitamin C than a lettuce leaf.

Flowers

Nasturtium seeds

When the flowers are over, look for the round seeds. You can dry these by leaving them on a sunny windowsill for a couple of weeks. Put them in the packet ready to plant next year. If you're really keen, you can pickle the seeds in vinegar. They taste like capers.

Make a gift

A pot or a hanging basket of nasturtiums would make a perfect present for the person who gave you this book.

Did you know?

What's in a name?

The name nasturtium comes from the Latin *nasturcium* from *nasus torquere*, meaning 'twisted nose' – because that's what you do when you taste its peppery leaves!

Nasturtium is actually the botanical name for watercress. Nasturtiums were originally known as Indian cress, but the nasturtium tag stuck as the common name for our orange flowers.

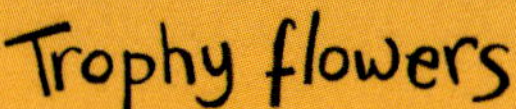

All the way from Peru

Nasturtiums are native to Peru. They were introduced into European gardens in the seventeenth century.

The Eden Project brings plants and people together.
It is dedicated to developing a greater understanding
of our shared global garden, encouraging us to
respect plants and protect them.

Other GROW YOUR OWN titles:

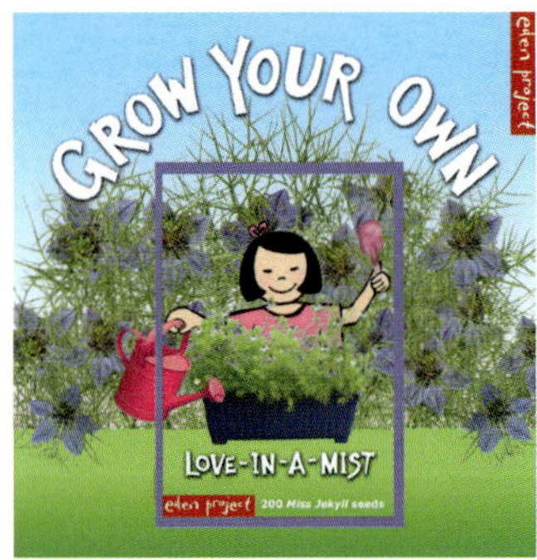

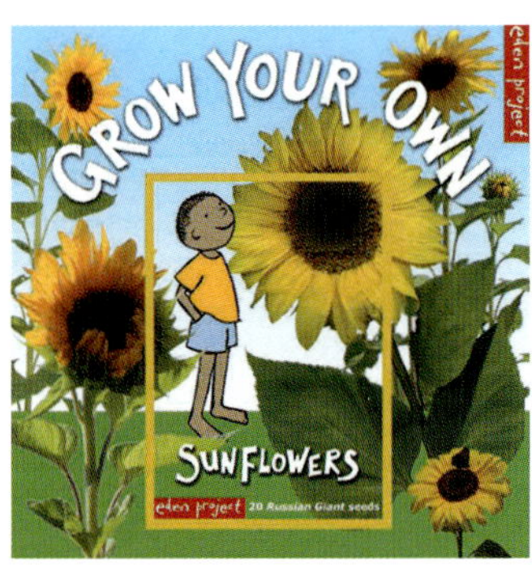

GROW YOUR OWN NASTURTIUMS
AN EDEN PROJECT BOOK 1 903 91937 1

Published in Great Britain in 2005 by Eden Project Books, an imprint of Transworld Publishers

1 3 5 7 9 10 8 6 4 2

Eden Project Books are published by Transworld Publishers, 61-63 Uxbridge Rd, London W5 5SA
A division of The Random House Group Ltd
In Australia by Random House Australia (Pty) Ltd 20 Alfred Street, Milsons Point, Sydney, NSW 2061, Australia
in New Zealand by Random House New Zealand Ltd 18 Poland Road, Glenfield, Auckland 10, New Zealand
and in South Africa by Random House (Pty) Ltd Endulini, 5A Jubilee Road, Parktown 2193, South Africa

THE RANDOM HOUSE GROUP Limited Reg. No. 954009

Printed and bound in Italy

A CIP catalogue record for this book is available from the British Library.

www.**kids**at**random**house.co.uk   www.edenproject.com